SPRING

A MENU FOR ALL SEASONS

SPRING

A Montecito Country Kitchen Cookbook

by Pascale Beale-Groom & Ann Marie Martorano-Powers

Foreword by Alyce Faye and John Cleese

PUBLISHED BY

Olive Tree Publishing
Santa Barbara, California 93108
PHONE (805) 569-1021
FAX (805) 969-5609

For cooking classes and merchandise:
www.montecitocountrykitchen.com
E-mail: montecitocountrykitchen@cox.net

A Menu For All Seasons I: Spring
A Montecito Country Kitchen Cookbook
by Pascale Beale-Groom & Ann Marie Martorano-Powers

First Edition

ISBN 0-9749603-0-6 (hardbound)
ISBN 0-9749603-1-4 (softbound)
Library of Congress Catalog Number: 2004101358

Design, Digital Production and Printing by Media 27, Inc., Santa Barbara, California

WWW.MEDIA27.COM

Printed and bound in the United States

Pour Mamie, Monique et Peter
les trois personnes qui m'ont donné l'art de vivre
et mes passions culinaires, et

Pour Steven, Olivia et Alexandre
les trois passions de ma vie

❤

To Grandma
for my inspiration,

To Scott, Stephanic, Fabrizio, Gregory, William and Emily
for enduring all my recipe testing, and

To Anabella
for the future

Menu for the
First day of Spring

Provencel Onion Tart
Fresh Herb Garden Salad

Vegetable, Olive and Caper
Stuffed Grilled Tuna
Polenta and Glazed Onions

Apricot Clafoutis

IN THE AUTUMN of 2000, my husband and I moved to Montecito for the winter months away from the cold of England.

It was my great luck almost immediately to learn of a cooking school called Montecito Country Kitchen. It was taught by two charming and delightful young women: Ann Marie, who is of Italian heritage, and Sicilian at that, and Pascale, who is of English and French heritage. This created a most interesting and sometimes hilarious dynamic between the two of them.

The classes are held in one of the older and more beautiful kitchens in Santa Barbara. A cozy collection of wannabe cooks, and sometimes rather skilled ones, gather round a large wooden work surface with marble inlay to learn the tricks of the trade. There, Ann Marie and Pascale instruct us in the ways of their European magic.

The first and most important item we were taught was *timing!* That means planning backwards, taking the longest and most difficult item first, and going forward until the entire meal is scheduled from start to finish.

Secondly, is the need to read through the recipe at least *twice* to make sure you know what is needed before your start. They also emphasize the *mise en place,* which means having all of your seasonal and quality ingredients prepared ahead of time and ready to go when you start cooking. This saves so much time and gives the cook great efficiency.

Et Voila! Your meal is presented at the perfect time and in gourmet style.

The ease and relaxation these skills give us are most apparent in the smiles of gratitude you see on our faces when we return the next week having prepared the perfect meal.

John and Alyce Faye in their kitchen in Montecito

MICHELLE SCHROBILGEN

Since my first introduction to these two whiz kids we have become very good friends, sharing many meals together. When we gather around a beautifully laid table, with a great glass of wine and a simple but elegant dinner. I do not think there could be happier times.

However, I suppose there might be one complaint. We have a small stable with quite a large vegetable garden. Quite often, I seem to observe our friends, Ann Marie and Pascale, gathering the harvest for the next cooking class. But even this gives us such a reward because of the tasty jars of goodies we receive after they have made their homemade preserves, chutneys, and olive oils.

I also have a confession to make: I do not like sweets! However, in this cook book, I found a dessert that I loved. It is the Lavender Pots de Crème with Lemon Thyme Meringues. The lavender lends a flavor unlike any other I have tasted. They are on page 59 and worth any effort. From a non-connoisseur of sweets, it is worth making.

If you, like me, can feel apprehensive about trying to cook a great meal, then this cook book of simple schedules, seasonal vegetables and crafty tips is absolutely the right book for you.

—ALYCE FAYE CLEESE

Ann Marie and Pascale have transformed my marriage. In the old days my wife had trouble preparing cornflakes. She used to boil them in the packets. Within a month of meeting our Mediterranean friends she was preparing delicious, original three course dinners, at the drop of a hat. Seriously, it is extraordinary what can be achieved by the steady acquisition of traditional European cooking skills. Thank you Ann Marie and Pascale.

—JOHN CLEESE

VIRGINIA WOOLF once said, "One cannot think well, love well, sleep well, if one has not dined well." Of all the great pleasures in life, gathering a group of friends around a dining table with good food, a robust glass of wine, laughter and lively conversation is surely the best. Whether it is over a simple bowl of pasta with a hearty tomato sauce, a traditional onion tart, a bowl of just-picked greens filled with the aroma of freshly-chopped basil, a piece of ciabatta, or baguette broken off to eat an oozing cheese, or to share a more formal meal, resplendent with, say, a risotto of wild mushrooms, a stuffed filet mignon, a Provençal rack of lamb and the like.

We both grew up in large, extended families for whom the dinner table was the nuclear core of life, mothers or grandmothers in the kitchen, children setting out the knives and forks, wafts of scented sauces drifting through the house. Through the years, food marked the milestones of growing up: the food of our childhood — buttery mashed potatoes, perhaps; the food in which we found solace — usually chocolate; the food of warmth and coziness — a rich *Boeuf en Daube*, a succulent *Osso Buco;* the food that captured our imagination — handmade ravioli, a soufflé — all are linked to the moments we first tasted them, be they the dishes we ate every day or those that came from special occasions. The common link was always our passion for food and those with whom we shared it.

This is a daily, engaging ritual for us, imbued in us by our forebears, handed down as an ongoing family tradition. This 'getting together,' parents with their children, generations at a family reunion or just good friends, creates a sense of love, communion and community. These traditions are celebrated in *A Menu For All Seasons.*

Ann Marie Pascoe

OUR GOAL in each of our classes, and by extension, this book, is to encourage everyone to get together in the kitchen, to have fun preparing a wonderful meal and to enjoy eating it. Cooking is a structured but creative medium which draws on and stimulates all senses. Foremost is the creation of the menu. Here is our recipe.

COOK WITH THE SEASONS: Use seasonal fruits and vegetables (organic if possible – local farmers markets are a great resource) in planning your meals. You will taste the difference in your food. The meals you cook will only be as good as the food you buy. "Old potatoes will taste like old potatoes."

BEGIN WITH THE HIGHLIGHT OF YOUR MENU: When creating menus we often walk around the farmers market or local markets for inspiration. There are many dishes that have come about as we spied some delicious looking mushrooms or salad or white asparagus.

Choosing your main course is often the easiest way to start. Decide if you want to serve fish or meat, poultry or pasta, a vegetarian dish or a stew, for example. This will give you the foundation of the entire meal. Once the key ingredient is chosen, decide if it needs an accompaniment. A stew filled with vegetables probably would not, but a roast chicken would be enhanced by some seasonal vegetables.

Don't feel obligated to add potatoes or rice to every dish. Many will stand alone; for example, you could serve the herbed racks of lamb on page 48 with just the haricots verts and it would be delicious.

BALANCE YOUR TASTES AND TEXTURES: Once you have chosen your main course, choose a first course that will complement it, something that will enliven the palate and that is usually light and enticing, but not so wild that it will jar one's tastes. Changes in temperature are also good for your palate. If you serve a very rich soup and then a stew, your guests will be overwhelmed, not only will they be full before you serve your masterpiece, but their taste buds will be dulled by the similar nature of each dish's texture. A light, fresh citrus salad would open their appetites before a heartier main course. Conversely, a small bowl of a savory soup would be wonderful before, perhaps, a grilled fish.

USE DIFFERENT COOKING METHODS: When choosing your dishes, bear in mind how they are prepared. If you decide to make a soufflé, then roast a chicken and then bake a tart, every item you have chosen needs to be cooked in the oven; a problem if you only have one oven. Using different cooking methods will ease preparation and will also enhance the differences in textures.

SAVOR WHAT YOU ARE PREPARING: Enjoy pleasing yourself and those for whom you are cooking. They will taste your enthusiasm in the food.

Top: Long-time students, Leesa Wilson-Goldmuntz and Alyce Faye Cleese, enjoying class. Bottom: Scott Powers, Ann Marie's husband, presiding over a class dinner.

THE KEY, we have found, to getting the most out of all your culinary efforts is twofold. The first is using the best possible and freshest seasonal fruits, vegetables and produce to hand. The second is timing. That is being able to get the whole meal on the table when you want it, without one dish being half-cooked whilst another is overdone. Many people have lamented to us over the past few years that they can roast a chicken but cannot get the vegetables, salads, etc., ready at the same time or that they get flustered at the very thought of having more than two people over for a meal. People tend to congregate in the kitchen, for it is truly the heart of the home, and we hope that you will have the same traffic jam around your kitchen counters, so give your guests a glass of wine, something to nibble on, and stop worrying.

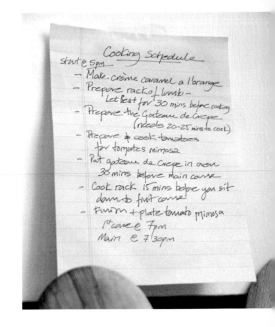

Every menu in this book emphasizes what we teach in every class: timing is the key to a successful meal. Here, you will find a simple technique to help with timing. You can create your own cooking schedules for any meal you prepare by adhering to the following:

COOKING SCHEDULE

1 Read the recipes 2 or 3 times before you start preparing and cooking to familiarize yourself with the procedure, the utensils and equipment you will need. This is especially true if you are making a new dish.

2 Gather all the ingredients you need for each dish *before* you start cooking. This will save time in the food preparation.

3 Decide at what time you wish to eat your MAIN course and write it down on the *bottom* of a piece of paper. This will form the basis of your schedule.

4 Working backwards from that time, you will be able to calculate how long you will need to *cook* your main course, e.g., if you are baking fish, you will often find that you are putting the fish in the oven only as you sit down to eat the first course, as fish, in most cases, needs so little time to cook.

5 Write down the time of your first course, allowing for 20-30 minutes between your first and main courses.

6 Then, work out how much time you need to prepare each of your dishes and allocate an order to them, preparing the dish that takes the longest time first. The majority of the time, this seems to be dessert. You will also find out that this means that you may be putting dishes in the oven, finishing sauces and so on, after your guests have arrived. Do not panic, and rest assured that if you have prepared the ingredients ahead of time and written down the order in which you are going to cook them, your meal will be a success.

Bearing the above in mind, feel free to mix and match the recipes in the book or cook just one dish.

White Asparagus with a Sauce Mousseline
Warm Grilled Duck and Watercress Salad
Lemon Tart

COOKING SCHEDULE

Starting 2 hours before you plan to eat your first course

- Prepare the dough first, as it has to rest for 1 hour.

- Prepare the filling for the tart.

- Prepare the watercress salad, but do not toss the salad until you are ready to serve it.

- Partially bake the tart shell and let cool.

- Finish the tart.

- Light the barbecue.

- Cook the asparagus.

- Prepare the sauce mousseline.

- Cook the duck – it will rest while you are eating the first course.

- Finish plating the duck salad after the first course.

NOTE:
The tart can be prepared earlier in the day but not the day before as the dough will become soggy.

WHITE ASPARAGUS WITH A SAUCE MOUSSELINE

I became enamored of them on my honeymoon in Italy and Austria, trying them at every opportunity in a variety of guises. Telling this story to Ann Marie inspired us to develop a sauce mousseline to complement these delicious and delicate stalks, the crème fraiche adding a little tanginess to balance the fresh, earthy taste of the asparagus. —PASCALE

Serves 8 people

2 lbs white asparagus – bottom half of the stems peeled and trimmed
4 egg yolks
2 tablespoons fresh lemon juice
Large pinch salt
10 oz (2 1/2 sticks) butter – clarified
White pepper
1/2 bunch parsley – finely chopped
1/2 bunch dill – finely chopped
4 tablespoons crème fraiche

THE KEY

WHITE ASPARAGUS NEED TO HAVE THEIR STALKS PEELED. HOWEVER, AS THE STALKS BREAK EASILY, THE BEST WAY TO DO THIS IS TO LAY THEM ON YOUR WORK SURFACE WITH THE TIPS FACING TOWARDS YOU. THEN, USING A VEGETABLE PEELER, PEEL THE STALKS, STARTING ABOUT 2 INCHES FROM THE TIP, MAKING SURE YOU HOLD THE STALKS FLAT ON THE SURFACE AS YOU WORK.

TO CLARIFY BUTTER, PLACE THE BUTTER IN A SMALL SAUCEPAN AND HEAT UNTIL IT LIQUIFIES SO THAT THE MILKY RESIDUE SINKS TO THE BOTTOM OF THE PAN. THE CLEAR LIQUID ABOVE IS THE CLARIFIED BUTTER. POUR THIS LIQUID OFF CAREFULLY INTO A SMALL BOWL.

1 Place the asparagus in a shallow pan filled with boiling water and cook until tender – 8 to 10 minutes. *Note: Check the asparagus before removing them to make sure they are cooked correctly – the white variety takes a little longer to cook than the green ones, which unlike the white ones, can be eaten al dente.*

2 Once they are cooked, drain and set aside on a platter.

3 Whilst the asparagus is cooking, prepare the sauce. Place the egg yolks, half the lemon juice and the salt in a medium-sized stainless steel bowl and whisk until the mixture is thick and creamy.

4 Place the bowl over a saucepan of simmering water, making sure the bottom of the bowl does not touch the water. Whisk the egg mixture until the egg just begins to thicken, being careful not to over cook the eggs – *otherwise they will quickly turn to scrambled eggs.*

5 Remove the bowl from the pan and very slowly whisk in the butter until it is all incorporated. Add the remaining lemon juice and the crème fraiche and whisk well so that the sauce is homogeneous. Add the freshly chopped herbs and the pepper and stir again. Serve immediately.

Origins

Asparagus, a royal treat, has grown in Europe since Roman times. The green variety graced the tables of Roman emperors and was a particular favorite of The Roi Soleil, King Louis XIV. White asparagus made its first appearance in France in the mid-1600s and has become a specialty of many European cuisines. They are grown under mounds of earth to protect the stems from sunlight, thus preventing them from turning green, and then painstakingly harvested by hand.

Origins

Watercress has been cultivated and consumed since Roman times for its purported medicinal and health-giving properties. It is high in vitamin C and Iron. It is said that it was used amongst other things to help combat baldness and to maintain a youthful appearance. Today it is more commonly used in salads and soups.

WARM GRILLED DUCK AND WATERCRESS SALAD

We were in Los Angeles recently on a culinary shopping expedition. After hours of searching for unusual pots, pans and other equipment, we adjourned to a wonderful Italian restaurant for a much-needed restorative lunch. We fell in love with a dish that combined pungent and peppery watercress with grilled duck. This recipe was inspired by that visit.

Serves 8 people

8 duck breasts

Salt and pepper

2 bunches watercress

1/2 lb mixed salad greens

Parsley – finely chopped

Dill – finely chopped

Chives – finely chopped

Olive oil

Dijon mustard

A good red wine vinegar – Jerez, if possible

1   Light your barbecue (use mesquite charcoal) 30 minutes before you plan to cook your duck – *of course if you have one of those gas-fired things, this is a moot point, just switch it on a few minutes before you are going to cook the duck.*

2   With a sharp knife, score the fatty side of the duck in a criss-cross pattern. Sprinkle with a little salt and pepper and set aside.

3   When the flames have subsided and the charcoal is glowing red, place the duck on the grill, fat side down, and cook for 7-8 minutes. *Note: Don't worry if the flames flare up again – it's from the duck fat.* Turn and cook a further 2-3 minutes on the other side. Remove the duck and let it rest for 5-10 minutes before slicing.

4   In a large salad bowl, place one large tablespoon of mustard. Drizzle in the olive oil slowly until the vinaigrette resembles the consistency of a light mayonnaise – usually about 2-3 tablespoons of olive oil are needed. Add in half a tablespoon of vinegar and whisk until the vinaigrette is homogeneous. Add salt and pepper to taste. *If you like your salad dressing with a little more kick, add a little more vinegar.*

5   Place the serving utensils in the bowl over the vinaigrette, and then place all the chopped herbs, covered by the mixed greens and the watercress, on top of the utensils. Do not let any of the greens sit in the vinaigrette. When you are ready to serve the salad, remove the serving utensils and toss the salad. Place a mound of the salad on each plate and then top with pieces of the sliced duck.

LEMON TART

We had been testing a meringue recipe the day before and, as a result, had lots of egg yolks left over. What better use for them than to make a tangy lemon tart. We experimented with our different family recipes and, after much puckering of lips, this was the favorite.

Serves 8-10 people

For the dough – enough to line a 12-inch tart pan (with a little left over) or enough to line eight individual 4-inch tart pans:

5 oz (1 1/3 cups) confectioner's sugar

1 lb (3 3/4 cups) flour

10 1/2 oz (2 1/2 sticks plus 1 tablespoon) unsalted butter

1 egg

4 oz (3/4 cup) crystallized ginger – chopped

Juice of 1/2 lemon

THE KEY

IN ALL OUR CLASSES WE ENCOURAGE EVERYONE TO BUY A WEIGHING MACHINE AS WEIGHING YOUR INGREDIENTS WILL PRODUCE THE BEST, MOST-ACCURATE AND CONSISTENT RESULTS (ESPECIALLY IN BAKING). WE HAVE FOUND THAT AS ALL MEASURING CUPS ARE NOT CREATED EQUAL – THEY TEND TO HAVE A SLIGHT VARIANCE BETWEEN MAKES – AND THAT NO TWO PEOPLE WILL FILL A CUP IN THE SAME MANNER, WEIGHING ITEMS SUCH AS FLOUR AND SUGAR IS THE BEST WAY TO GO. FOR THIS REASON WE LIST THE WEIGHT FIRST AND THE EQUIVALENT CUP MEASUREMENT SECOND.

1 Place all the ingredients in the bowl of a food processor and pulse until just combined. Remove the dough from the bowl, and place onto a large piece of plastic wrap and flatten out a little – the dough will be slightly sticky. Wrap it up and refrigerate for 1 hour before using. *Please note that it will still be soft after 1 hour.*

2 Preheat the oven to 400 degrees.

3 Roll the dough out between two sheets of plastic wrap. Remove the top sheet of plastic wrap. Pick up the rolled-out dough with the second sheet of plastic wrap and invert it into a buttered 12-inch tart pan. If you are making individual tarts, cut the rolled-out dough into eight equal parts and proceed in the same manner. Remove the second sheet of plastic wrap. Trim the edges of the dough and then prick the dough with the tines of a fork. Cover the dough with a little foil and then place pie weights or beans over the foil. Bake in the oven for 10 minutes so that the dough is a pale golden color. Remove from the oven and after removing the pie weights, let it cool down.

Origins

Lemons have been cultivated for over 2000 years, originating, it is thought, in the Indus valley. Though first widely used in Arabic cuisines, its uses over time have ranged from reddening ladies' lips in the French royal courts to fighting scurvy amongst sailors in the days before refrigeration. The variety known as Meyer Lemons was brought to America from China by Mr. Meyer in 1908. This tart is especially good using these lemons, if you can get your hands on them.

For the filling:

Grated zest and juice of 4 lemons

4 whole eggs

3 egg yolks

6 oz (3/4 cup plus 1 tablespoon) sugar

3 oz (3/4 stick) butter – melted

THE KEYS

TAKE EXTRA CARE NOT TO LET THE FILLING BOIL – YOUR PATIENCE IN SLOWLY STIRRING THE EGG YOLK MIXTURE WILL BE WELL REWARDED WITH A SILKY, LUSCIOUS TART.

ROLLING THE LEMONS BACKWARDS AND FORWARDS ON A COUNTER TOP WHILE PRESSING DOWN ON THEM, WILL HELP EXTRACT MORE JUICE FROM EACH LEMON.

1   Place the lemon juice and zests in a large bowl. Place the bowl over a saucepan of simmering water and heat up the lemon juice until warm to the touch.

2   Whisk in the whole eggs and then the egg yolks, being careful not to let the mixture boil, as this will cause the eggs to curdle. Add in the sugar and melted butter, stirring until the mixture thickens enough to coat the back of a spoon. This will take a little time, be patient and do not turn the heat up.

3   Pour the finished lemon mixture into the partially baked tart and cook a further 10 minutes or until the tart is golden brown.

Bresaola and Arugula Salad with Shaved Parmesan
Salmon and Spinach Towers with a Spicy Tomato Sauce
Gâteau de Baumes de Venise

COOKING SCHEDULE

Starting 2 hours before you plan to eat your first course

- Make the gâteau de Baumes de Venise (this can be made up to 24 hours in advance).

- Make the salmon and spinach towers but do not cook them yet.

- Make the spicy tomato sauce.

- Put the salmon towers in the oven (they need 30 minutes to cook) so time this 35 minutes before you plan to eat your main course.

- Make the bresaola salad.

BRESAOLA AND ARUGULA SALAD WITH SHAVED PARMESAN

I discovered bresaola during a visit to Switzerland and couldn't stop eating it. On my return to California, I found fresh arugula in my father's garden, and thinking that it would go well with the cured beef, created this version of the traditional Italian salad. The marriage between the two is delicious.

—ANN MARIE

Serves 8 people

1 lb (approximately 32 slices) bresaola – thinly sliced

1/4 lb mixed greens

1/2 lb fresh baby arugula

1/4 lb Parmesan – very thinly sliced or shavings of Parmesan

1/2 cup walnuts – chopped

Extra virgin olive oil

1 tablespoon walnut oil

1 tablespoon balsamic vinegar

Coarse salt

Freshly ground black pepper

1   Lay out the bresaola on a large serving platter or four slices on each individual serving plate.

2   In a mixing bowl, place the mixed greens, arugula and walnuts and toss to combine all the ingredients.

3   In a separate small bowl, pour in the oils, the balsamic vinegar, a good pinch of salt, and 5 or 6 good turns of black pepper and whisk to combine. Pour the dressing over the salad greens and toss again to coat well.

4   Place all the greens on top of the bresaola in the middle of the serving platter or the individual plates and top with the shaved Parmesan.

THE KEY

BUY ONLY THE FRESHEST BRESAOLA. IT MUST BE MOIST IN TEXTURE AND LOOK DARK RED. IF THE BEEF LOOKS A LITTLE BROWN IT IS PAST ITS PRIME AND WILL TEND TO BE DRY.

Origins

Bresaola is a type of air dried beef from the Italian Alps. Arugula: Italians call it rucola or rughetta —
roquette in France and often in England. In pure Sicilian dialect it is known as arugula, and as it was introduced
to America by Sicilian immigrants, it is known by that name in this country.

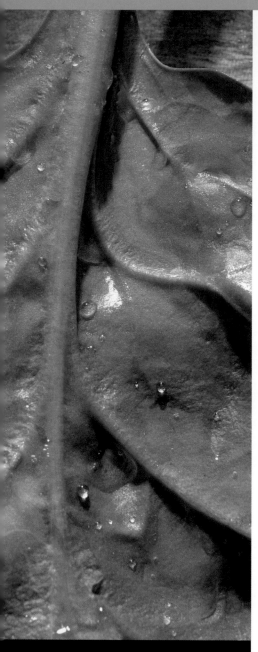

SALMON AND SPINACH TOWERS WITH A SPICY TOMATO SAUCE

It was one of those days when you get home late from work and think you'll just throw something together, an omelet maybe or a soufflé, my husband Steven's favorite. I opened the fridge and realized that all we had was one small filet of salmon, about half a pound of spinach and 2 eggs. Not enough for a soufflé evidently, but enough to make a miniature version of a spinach mousse we both liked and just enough to create the base for this dish. Thus the little "towers" came about. —PASCALE

Serves 8 people

Salmon and Spinach Towers

2 1/2 lbs salmon filet

1 tablespoon fennel seeds

Salt and pepper

1 lb baby spinach

1 (about 2 tablespoons) knob butter

3 eggs

2 tablespoons cream

THE KEY

TO HELP INVERT THE SALMON AND SPINACH TOWERS, RUN A THIN KNIFE AROUND THE INSIDE EDGE OF THE RAMEKIN TO LOOSEN THE MOUSSE.

1   Preheat the oven to 400 degrees.

2   Thinly slice the salmon into 1/2 inch thick strips and place them in a bowl. Add the fennel seeds and a little salt and pepper. Stir to combine.

3   In a large saucepan, melt the knob of butter over medium heat. When it is foaming, add the spinach and cook until it is just wilted. Add in the 2 tablespoons of cream and stir again to combine.

4   Pour the spinach in a blender and add the eggs. Puree the spinach and eggs in the blender until smooth.

5   You will need a 4-inch wide ramekin for each person. Oil each ramekin with a little olive oil. Take the salmon strips and form them into a circle, gradually overlapping each one so that it will form a disk that is large enough to fit the bottom of the ramekin. Pour the spinach mousse over the salmon so that it comes about 3/4 inch above the salmon.

6   Place the ramekins in a baking dish and fill the baking dish with water so that the water comes two thirds of the way up the sides of the ramekins. Place in the oven and bake for 30 minutes.

7   Remove from the oven and carefully invert onto the middle of a warmed dinner plate. The salmon towers should invert easily and slide out. Serve immediately with the sauce.

Origins

Spinach originally came from Persia and has been used in cooking since the Middle Ages across Europe. Spinach recipes exist from Chaucer's time and it is quite possible that the pilgrims ate soups of braised greens and spinach on their way to Canterbury. Old manuscript editions of 14th and 15th century cookbooks, notably the *Curyean Inglysch*, contain some of these recipes.

Spicy Tomato Sauce

Serves 8 people

Olive oil

1 large yellow onion – peeled and thinly
    sliced

6 shallots – peeled and thinly sliced

3 cloves garlic – peeled and crushed

8 large tomatoes – chopped into small
    pieces

1 pinch saffron

1 pinch cayenne pepper

4 oz (2/3 cup) black Niçoises olives –
    pitted and chopped

Salt and pepper

Freshly chopped dill

THE KEY

DO NOT ADD THE TOMATOES UNTIL THE
ONIONS ARE SOFT, AS THEIR ACIDITY WILL
STOP THE COOKING OF THE ONIONS. IF YOU
HAVE EVER HAD A TOMATO SAUCE WITH
'CRUNCHY' ONIONS IN IT, IT IS BECAUSE THE
TOMATOES WERE ADDED TOO SOON!

1   In a large saucepan, pour in a little
olive oil, and add the shallots, onion
and garlic. Sauté for 8-10 minutes or
until the onions are translucent and
soft.

2   Add the tomatoes, saffron, the
pinch of cayenne pepper, and cook
for 10 minutes. When the sauce has
started to thicken and the tomatoes
have lost most of their water, add the
olives, salt and pepper. Cook over low
heat for a further 15 minutes. Taste the
sauce at this point. If you want it to be
a little spicier, add a little more cayenne
pepper.

3   Just before serving the sauce, add
the freshly chopped dill, stir once more
and use whilst hot.

GÂTEAU DE BAUMES DE VENISE

Whilst reading an old book on Provençal desserts, I came across a cake using Baumes de Venise. As this fortified wine was a long-time favorite of my grandmother's, I was intrigued and adapted the recipe to the cake we have here. Alas, my lovely "Mamie" had passed away before I could make it for her. This cake is a tribute to her and to all the 'delices' she used to make for me as a child.

—PASCALE

Serves 8-10 people

4 extra large eggs – separated

4 oz (1 stick) butter

4 oz (1/2 cup plus 1 1/2 tablespoons) sugar

2 tablespoons olive oil

Zest of 2 lemons and the juice of 1/2 lemon

Zest of 1 orange

8 oz (1 3/4 cups) all purpose unbleached flour

1/2 teaspoon salt

1 1/3 cups Baumes de Venise

1 lb grapes – you can use red or white seedless varieties

1 tablespoon light brown sugar

1 tablespoon sugar – mix with the light brown sugar above in a small bowl

2 oz (1/2 stick) butter

1   Preheat the oven to 400 degrees. Coat a 10-12 inch cake tin with a removable bottom with olive oil. Set aside.

2   Whisk the egg whites until they hold firm peaks. Set aside.

3   Place the butter in the bowl of an electric mixer and beat until creamy. Add the sugar and beat 1 minute more, then add the olive oil and beat until smooth. Add the zests and juice, and then add in the egg yolks one at a time and beat until you have a smooth mixture.

4   Add the flour, salt and wine to the egg yolk mixture and whisk until well combined and smooth.

5   Gently fold the egg whites into the batter. Pour it into the prepared cake tin, and drop the grapes over the surface. Combine the brown sugar and sugar in a small bowl. Sprinkle the mixed sugars over the surface and dot the sugar with little knobs of butter.

6   Bake the cake for 35-40 minutes or until a knife inserted into the center of the cake comes out clean. Remove from the oven and serve at room temperature.

Pascale's son Alexandre helping with the gâteau.

Origins

Baumes de Venise, a sweet wine, made from Muscat grapes, is named after a town in the Vaucluse region of France.

Tarte a l'Onion with a Fresh Herb Garden Salad
Vegetable, Olive and Caper Stuffed Grilled Tuna
Polenta with a Black Olive Sauce
Apricot Clafoutis

COOKING SCHEDULE

Starting 2 hours before you plan to eat your first course

- Make the tarte dough (it has to rest for at least 30 minutes).

- Make the clafoutis and bake (you can make this earlier in the day if you wish, but do not refrigerate it).

- Cook the onions for the tarte.

- Finish the tarte and bake it.

- Prepare the tuna – but do not cook it yet.

- Make the fresh herb salad.

- Heat the stock for the polenta just before sitting down to the first course.

- Grill the tuna between the first and second courses, as it only takes 5 minutes to grill.

- Finish the polenta just before serving the main course.

TARTE A L'ONION WITH A FRESH HERB GARDEN SALAD

This tarte holds a special place in my heart for it was one of the first dishes I made entirely by myself and, for that reason, was featured in the first class of the cooking school. It also has a long family history, made by many generations. This is my mother's version. She was introduced to it as a young girl by her aunt, Tante Lilette, who used to make it during the summer holidays on the Cote d'Azur. This tarte, called a 'Pissaladiere' in France, is a specialty of that region. The name is derived from the condiment Pissalat, (made up of an anchovy purée and spiced with thyme, bay leaves, cloves and olive oil) which traditionally covers the onion layer of the tarte. Outside of Nice, you often see a latticework of anchovy filets covering the tarte. I like to dot mine with a lot of black Niçoises olives. The anchovies are optional.

—PASCALE

This recipe will serve 8 people for a large tarte or 6-8 people for individual tartes.

Short crust pastry

9 oz (2 cups) unbleached all purpose flour

1 large egg

5 1/2 oz (1 1/3 sticks) slightly softened butter – cut up into small pieces

1 teaspoon cold milk (if needed)

Pinch of salt

1 Preheat oven to 400 degrees.

2 Butter either a 9-inch fluted tarte pan with a removable bottom or each of the individual moulds.

3 Prepare pastry (we have listed two methods).

Traditional method

a In a large ceramic or metal bowl place all the sifted flour. Make a well in the center of the flour and add the whole egg, all the butter and the pinch of salt.

b Using the tips of your fingers, slowly incorporate all the ingredients drawing the flour from the outside of the bowl towards the center. Once incorporated, the ingredients should resemble coarse breadcrumbs.

c Using your whole hand and the palm of your hand, bring the dough together to form a ball. If the dough seems a little dry, add a touch of the milk – using as little as possible. The dough should be smooth but not too tacky to the touch.

d Wrap the dough in plastic wrap and refrigerate it until ready to use. You can make the dough ahead of time and leave in the fridge. You will need to remove the dough from the fridge approximately 20 minutes before using it.

Food processor method

a   Place all the ingredients in the bowl of the food processor fitted with a metal blade.

b   Use repeated pulses until the mixture resembles coarse breadcrumbs.

c   Add a little of the milk, as necessary, if the dough seems too dry. Use longer pulses until the dough has formed a ball. The texture of the dough made in the food processor is different to that made by hand. It will look smoother and be slightly tackier to the touch.

d   Wrap the dough in plastic wrap and refrigerate it until ready to use. You can make the dough ahead of time and leave in the fridge. You will need to remove the dough from the fridge approximately 20 minutes before using it.

THE KEY

LETTING THE DOUGH REST IN THE REFRIGERATOR ONCE YOU HAVE MADE IT MAKES ROLLING IT OUT EASIER.

For the onions:

2 tablespoons olive oil

6-8 large yellow onions – peeled, cut in half and sliced thinly

Salt and pepper to taste

Black Niçoises olives

Whilst the dough is resting, prepare the onion mixture.

1   In a large heavy saucepan heat the olive oil over medium heat. Add all the sliced onions and cook over low to medium heat for 30 minutes. The onions should be a light gold color. Do not brown them. Add salt and pepper to taste. The onions, when ready, will have an almost creamy texture to them.

Assembling the tarte:

1   Remove the pastry from the fridge. On a lightly floured board roll out the pastry dough in an even manner to the size of the mould. If you are making individual tartes, roll out the pastry and cut out the dough to fit the individual moulds. Place the dough in the tarte pan(s).

2   Trim the edges of the dough with a sharp knife and then prick the dough in the bottom of the tarte pan(s) with the tines of a fork. (This prevents the dough from rising into ungainly bumps whilst it is cooking.)

3   Pour all of the onion mixture over the dough and spread evenly with the back of a fork or spoon so that the onion mixture forms an even layer over the pastry. Grind some fresh black pepper over the top of the onions.

4   Place the tarte in the center of the oven and bake for 25-30 minutes. Both the pastry and the onions should be a golden brown color.

5   Remove the tarte from its mould and let it cool slightly.

6   Dot the onion tarte with the black olives. Serve with a fresh green salad.

THE KEYS

THE TRUE SUCCESS OF THIS TARTE LIES IN THE COOKING — THE VERY SLOW COOKING — OF THE ONIONS. IF YOU RUSH THEM, THEY WILL BE TOO CRUNCHY.

AFTER WORKING WITH ONIONS, ALWAYS SMELL THE WORK SURFACES ON WHICH YOU CHOPPED THEM — NOTHING IS WORSE THAN PREPARING ANOTHER DISH, ESPECIALLY SWEET ONES, ON A SURFACE THAT HAS NOT BEEN PROPERLY WIPED DOWN AFTER CHOPPING ONIONS. IF THE SMELL IS PARTICULARLY STUBBORN, SQUEEZE A LITTLE LEMON JUICE OVER THE WORK SURFACE, SCRUB IT DOWN AND THEN WASH WITH HOT WATER. CHECK YOUR KNIVES IN THE SAME MANNER.

Fresh Herb Garden Salad

In much of the Mediterranean a fresh salad is served with almost every meal. This is one of our favorites.

Serves 8 people

Dijon mustard

Olive oil

A good aged red wine or sherry vinegar of your choice

Salt & pepper to taste

Mixed field greens – preferably with arugula in the mix – for 8 people

Fresh dill – finely chopped

Fresh basil – finely chopped

Fresh chives – finely chopped

Fresh Italian parsley – finely chopped

Fresh oregano – finely chopped (use less of this herb as it is quite strong)

Fresh cilantro – optional

1 In a large salad bowl, place one large tablespoon of mustard. Drizzle in the olive oil slowly, whisking all the time, until the vinaigrette resembles the consistency of a light mayonnaise – usually about 2-3 tablespoons of olive oil are needed. Add in one tablespoon of vinegar and whisk until the vinaigrette is homogeneous. Add salt and pepper to taste.

2 Place the serving utensils in the bowl over the vinaigrette, and then place all the chopped herbs, covered by the mixed greens on top of the utensils. Do not let any of the greens sit in the vinaigrette. When you are ready to serve the salad, remove the serving utensils and toss the salad.

THE KEYS

PEOPLE'S TASTES IN VINAIGRETTES VARY CONSIDERABLY – THIS RECIPE CAN BE MADE MORE OR LESS STRONG BY ADDING MORE OR LESS MUSTARD AND VINEGAR. IF TOO MUCH OLIVE OIL IS ADDED, THE VINAIGRETTE WILL SEPARATE.

CHOPPING BASIL: STACK THE BASIL LEAVES IN A SMALL PILE WITH THE LARGEST ON THE BOTTOM AND THEN ROLL THEM UP TIGHTLY LIKE A SMALL CIGAR. USING A SHARP KNIFE, FINELY CHOP THE LEAVES WITH A SWIFT UP AND DOWN MOTION, KEEPING THE TIP OF YOUR KNIFE ON THE CHOPPING BOARD AT ALL TIMES. YOU WILL HAVE FINE RIBBONS OF BASIL USING THIS METHOD.

VEGETABLE, OLIVE AND CAPER STUFFED GRILLED TUNA

A good friend of ours returned from his 40th birthday fishing trip with well over 1000 lbs of tuna. Realizing that he couldn't possibly consume all of it himself, he delivered large quantities to all his friends around town. We were lucky enough to receive some fabulous pieces, so we called up a few people and had a tuna dinner. It was prepared in three different ways, including this dish which reminded us of tuna dinners eaten halfway around the world on the shores of the Mediterranean.

Serves 8 people

Olive oil

2 onions – finely chopped

4 garlic cloves – finely chopped

1 bunch green onions – finely chopped

3 tablespoons fennel seeds

1 zucchini – finely chopped

2 lbs filet of tuna – 1 1/2 lbs cut into thin slices, the rest cut into small cubes

4 tomatoes – finely chopped

6 oz (1 cup) black Niçoises olives – finely chopped

3 tablespoons capers – roughly chopped

Salt and pepper

THE KEY

ALWAYS SERVE FISH DISHES, INDEED ALL HOT DISHES, ON WARM PLATES. A COLD PLATE UNDER A DELICATE FISH DISH WILL GO A LONG WAY TO RUINING ALL YOUR HARD WORK AS THE FISH AND ANY ACCOMPANYING SAUCE WILL BE STONE COLD BY THE TIME YOU GET IT TO THE TABLE. PLATES CAN BE KEPT WARM IN AN OVEN AT 200 DEGREES OR A SINK FILLED WITH HOT WATER. IT IS ABSOLUTELY WORTH THE EFFORT.

1 Pour a little olive oil in a large skillet over medium high heat. When hot, add in the chopped onions, garlic, green onions, and fennel seeds and cook for 3-4 minutes until just soft and lightly golden. Then add the zucchini and cook for a further 5 minutes until soft and golden.

2 Add the 1/2 lb of chopped tuna to the mixture and cook for a further 60 seconds until the tuna pieces are barely cooked through. Remove from heat.

3 Place all the remaining ingredients into a large bowl and mix them well. Add the warm onion/tuna mixture to the bowl and combine well again. Set aside.

4 Lay the sliced tuna on a work surface. Spoon a large tablespoon of the onion mixture into the middle of the tuna slices and roll them up, completely covering the filling. Place the rolled up tuna onto a square piece of parchment paper and wrap it up tightly. Cover each roll with foil and wrap tightly again to form little "sausages." Place these packages on a hot grill and cook for 4-5 minutes turning them once or twice. You can also cook these in the oven at 400 degrees for 6 minutes.

POLENTA WITH A BLACK OLIVE SAUCE

My earliest memory of polenta, as a young child, is sweet polenta made by my great-grandmother, Octaviana, who emigrated from Asti in Italy. She used to stand in front of her tiny stove, making large quantities of her creamy, honey sweetened polenta for her 16 great-grandchildren. It was heavenly. However, the Sicilian side of the family had quite a different version. Grandma Lena made for her 12 children (I am one of her 46 great grandchildren) a very firm savory polenta which was mopped up with a beefy tomato sauce. This version is of the creamy savory variety.

—ANN MARIE

As a child, I did not like polenta. Even recently, I was not a great fan until, that is, I met Ann Marie who makes the most wonderful, creamy polenta. It has transformed my appreciation of this dish to the point where it now makes regular appearances on our dinner table. —PASCALE

Serves 8 people

Grandma Lena at home in Los Angeles, 1954

Origins

Polenta, a cornmeal dish originating in northern Italy in the 16th century, has inspired some people to go to great lengths to celebrate its virtues, amongst them a group in the 19th century called Prima Patria, Poi Polenta – "First the mother country, then Polenta!"

❤

For the black olive sauce:

Olive oil

1 tablespoon butter

1 red onion – finely chopped

16 oz (2 2/3 cups) black Niçoises olives – pitted and finely chopped

For the polenta:

2 cups milk

2 cups chicken stock

1/2 cup quick cooking polenta

Coarse salt and freshly ground white pepper to taste

2 roma tomatoes – diced for garnish

1 Pour a little olive oil and add the butter into a medium-sized saucepan placed over medium heat. Add the red onion and cook for 10 minutes so that the onions are very soft. Add the chopped olives, stir well to combine and cook for a further 2-3 minutes. Cover and keep warm.

2 In another medium-sized saucepan bring the milk and chicken stock to a simmer. Be careful that it does not boil over. Slowly whisk in the polenta and cook over low heat for 5 minutes, stirring constantly, until the mixture is thick and creamy. Season with the salt and pepper. Serve at once with a spoonful of the warm olive sauce topped with a sprinkle of the chopped tomatoes.

APRICOT CLAFOUTIS

This is one of those dishes that reminds me of my childhood. Both my grandmother and my aunt, Marie-France, with whom we spent many a family holiday, made fabulous traditional cherry Clafoutis. Over the years, I have tried, virtually, all fruit in the creamy custard base. This one is the family favorite. —PASCALE

Serves 8-10 people

3 cups milk

8 oz (1 1/4 cups) sugar

1 vanilla bean – split lengthwise

3 oz (2/3 cup) unbleached all purpose flour

5 large eggs

2 lbs apricots – stoned and cut into small pieces

3 tablespoons Grand Marnier or cognac (optional)

1 Preheat oven to 400 degrees.

2 In a medium-sized saucepan heat the milk with the sugar and the vanilla bean. Stir until the sugar has completely dissolved. Set aside.

3 In a separate bowl place the flour and then whisk in one egg at a time. You should have a completely smooth batter. Slowly stir in the milk mixture. The batter should be very liquid but free of any lumps. Set aside.

4 Place the apricot pieces in a shallow round baking dish and add the Grand Marnier or cognac (if using). Toss with a spoon until all the pieces are coated.

5 Pour the batter over the fruit and fill the baking dish.

6 Place in the center of the oven and bake for 45 minutes. The clafoutis is done when you jiggle the pan and it is set. The top should appear golden brown. Serve at room temperature. This dessert is also great the next day, especially with a cup of coffee!

Origins

Clafoutis originally came from the Limousin region of France. The word clafoutis comes from the old Provençal dialect, where the word *clafir* means 'to fill.'

Carrot and Shallot Soup with Chervil Cream
Roasted Cornish Hens and Apricots with an Apricot Glaze
Asparagus Amandine
Amaretto Ice Cream with Kahlúa Almond Tuiles

COOKING SCHEDULE

Earlier in the day

- Prepare the ice cream and freeze.
- Make the tuiles (from start to finish).

Starting 2 hours before you plan to eat your first course

- Make the soup (except the last step of the chervil cream).
- Prepare the Cornish hens with apricots and place in the oven 1 hour 15 minutes before you wish to eat them.
- Prepare the asparagus amandine just before you sit down to eat the first course.
- Finish the chervil cream and serve the soup.

CARROT AND SHALLOT SOUP WITH CHERVIL CREAM

Serves 8 people

1 lb carrots – peeled and chopped into 1-inch pieces

1 oz (1/4 stick) butter

5 cups roasted chicken stock (you can also use vegetable stock if you wish – see page 66)

Salt

1 teaspoon olive oil

5 shallots – peeled and finely sliced

1 cup cream

1 large bunch fresh chervil

Black pepper

1   Steam the carrots until they are very tender. Remove them from the steamer and then purée them in a food processor with the butter and a good pinch of salt. The purée should be very smooth. Add two cups of the chicken stock (or vegetable stock if using) and purée again. Pour all of the carrot purée into a large saucepan and add the remaining stock of your choice. Bring to a simmer.

2   Whilst the soup is simmering, pour the olive oil into a small saucepan placed over medium heat. Add the sliced shallots and cook for 4-5 minutes so that they are golden brown and releasing their fragrance. Add the chopped chervil to the shallots and cook for 1 minute, then add the cream. Reduce the heat to low and stir well to infuse the cream with the chervil.

3   Pour the carrot soup into warmed soup bowls and then swirl some of the chervil cream into the middle of the soup. Serve hot.

THE KEY

INSERTING A CORK UNDER THE HANDLE OF A SAUCEPAN LID WILL ALLOW YOU TO PICK THE LID UP WITHOUT BURNING YOUR FINGERS. USED WINE CORKS ARE PERFECT FOR SMALLER LIDS, AND CHAMPAGNE CORKS ARE GREAT FOR LARGE STOCKPOT LIDS.

ROASTED CORNISH HENS AND APRICOTS WITH AN APRICOT GLAZE AND ASPARAGUS AMANDINE

This recipe came about because of an overabundance of apricots. We had just finished making 50 pounds of apricot jam when a neighbor delivered a huge box of yet more apricots. We preserved some in cognac, we made apricot Clafoutis, apricot tarts, apricot cakes, and still had a few left over, and so decided to try them with the Cornish hens we were roasting. The effect of the apricots on the hens is luscious. It is a shame the apricot season is so short, as we could eat this dish all year round.

Serves 8

16 firm ripe apricots – cut in half

1/2 cup cognac or brandy

1/2 cup shallots – chopped

3 tablespoons butter

4 oz (1 cup) pistachios – chopped

Salt and pepper to taste

4 Cornish hens

2 cups apricot jam

1   Preheat the oven to 400 degrees.

2   Place the apricots and cognac in a bowl and let stand for 10 minutes. Drain the apricots, reserving the liquid.

3   In a sauté pan, sauté the shallots in the butter until translucent. Stir in the salt, pepper, pistachios and apricots and combine well. Cook for a further 3 minutes. Remove from the heat.

4   Place the Cornish hens in the roasting pan and coat each one with the apricot jam. Then spoon the apricot/shallot mixture around them. Place in the center of the oven and bake for 1 hour.

5   Remove the game hens from the oven and place them on a carving board. Let them rest for 10 minutes before carving. Warm 8 dinner plates in the oven.

6   Spoon 4 apricot halves onto each of the warmed dinner plates.

7   Stir the reserved apricot liquid (from step 2) into the roasting pan and reduce the pan juices over a medium hot stove until lightly thickened. Cut the game hens in half, place one half on each plate alongside the apricots and pour a little of the pan juices over the top. Serve with the asparagus amandine.

Asparagus Amandine

1 1/2 lbs asparagus – cleaned and cut into 2 inch long pieces

1 oz (1/2 cup) sliced almonds

1 tablespoon butter

Salt and pepper

1   In a medium pan, melt the butter over medium heat and sauté the almonds for 2 minutes. Set aside.

2   Place the asparagus in a large pan filled with boiling water. Cook for 4 minutes. Drain and set aside.

3   Return the pan with the almonds to the heat and add the asparagus. Stir to combine and cook for a further 3 minutes. The asparagus should be green and slightly crunchy.

THE KEY
MAKE SURE YOU DON'T OVER COOK THE ASPARAGUS. THEY SHOULD BE AL DENTE AS IT CREATES A LOVELY CONTRAST WITH THE SUCCULENCE OF THE CORNISH HENS.

AMARETTO ICE CREAM WITH KAHLÚA ALMOND TUILES

Amaretto Ice Cream

Serves 8-10 people

1 2/3 cups whole milk

1 teaspoon vanilla extract

6 large egg yolks

5 oz (3/4 cup) sugar

1/8 teaspoon salt

2 cups heavy cream – chilled

1/3 cup Amaretto

1   In a medium-sized saucepan, over medium heat, bring the milk and the vanilla extract just to a simmer.

2   In the top of a double boiler or a medium-sized stainless steel bowl, whisk the yolks and the sugar and salt for 3-4 minutes until pale yellow. Gradually whisk in the hot milk. Place the top of the double boiler or the stainless steel bowl over a pan of simmering (not boiling) water and cook, whisking constantly for 8-10 minutes or until the custard is thick enough to coat the back of a spoon.

3   Remove the bowl or top of the double boiler from the water and then stir the cream into the warm custard mixture. Add the Amaretto and stir to distribute it evenly in the mixture.

4   Chill the mixture for 30 minutes, or until cool, and then pour into the ice cream maker and freeze according to the manufacturer's directions.

THE KEY

MAKE SURE THAT THE BOWL OF YOUR ICE CREAM MACHINE IS *VERY* COLD. PLACING IT IN THE FREEZER OVERNIGHT IS THE BEST. IF IT IS NOT COLD ENOUGH, THE ICE CREAM DOES NOT SET PROPERLY.

Kahlúa Almond Tuiles

Makes approximately 25 tuiles

1 egg

3 oz (1/2 cup) superfine sugar

1 1/2 tablespoon safflower oil

1 1/2 tablespoon butter – melted

3/4 oz (2 tablespoons) unbleached flour

1 teaspoon Kahlúa

2 oz (2/3 cup) sliced almonds

1   Place a rack in the middle of the oven and preheat to 350 degrees.

2   Place the egg and sugar in a medium-sized bowl and whisk together until creamy. Pour in the oil, melted butter, flour and Kahlúa and stir to combine well. Then carefully fold in the almonds.

3   Line two cookie sheets with Silpat or make sure the pans are well oiled. Place teaspoonfuls of the almond mixture, at least 3 inches apart on the prepared pans. Before baking them, make sure you have a thin metal flexible spatula and at least 1 or 2 rolling pins ready at hand. *Note: The rolling pins are used to curl the tuiles.*

4   Bake each cookie sheet separately for 6-7 minutes or until golden brown. Remove the pan and immediately lift each cookie very carefully off the sheet using the spatula and drape over the rolling pin. They will set in just a few minutes. Repeat with the second pan.

THE KEY

SHAPE THE TUILES AS SOON AS YOU REMOVE THEM FROM THE OVEN. IF YOU WAIT TOO LONG THEY WILL NOT FORM THE SHAPE YOU DESIRE.

THESE TUILES ARE BEST SERVED THE DAY THEY ARE MADE AS THEY ARE VERY FRAGILE.

Origins

Tuiles are so named as they resemble curved roof tiles, called *tuiles* in France.

Amaretto is an almond liqueur made in Italy in Serano since 1525. The story behind the murano glass bottled liqueur is enchanting. Artist Bernardino Luini, of the Da Vinci School, was commissioned to paint a fresco of the Madonna. After a lengthy search, he found a beautiful young woman to pose for him, the daughter of an innkeeper who, after months of posing for the artist, fell deeply in love with him. As a tribute to her love, she made this sweet almond-scented liqueur. The Disaranno Company has been making the liqueur ever since, using a recipe now unchanged for almost 500 years.

Zucchini Mousse with a Salsa di Pomodoro
Grilled Fish in Grape Leaves with a Dill Butter Sauce
Timbales of Rice with Fresh Herbs
Peach Tart and Lavender Crème Anglaise

COOKING SCHEDULE

Starting 2 hours before you plan to eat your first course

- Prepare and refrigerate the tart dough.

- Prepare the zucchini mousse up to step 7.

- Make the crème anglaise – this can also be made earlier in the day if you wish.

- Finish the peach tart and bake.

- Make the salsa di pomodoro.

- Prepare the fish in grape leaves.

- Make the timbales of rice.

- Bake the zucchini mousse 45 minutes before the start of the first course.

- Make the dill sauce.

- Plate the zucchini mousse.

- Place fish on grill just as you sit down to eat the first course.

ZUCCHINI MOUSSE WITH A SALSA DI POMODORO

We had a mountain of courgettes (zucchini) in the kitchen and were inventing different ways to cook them. This is one of the dishes we came up with. The colors are very pretty and it also makes a great main course for lunch. Ann Marie created a delicious salsa di pomodoro (a thick tomato sauce) to complement the mousse.

—PASCALE

Serves 8

Zucchini Mousse

Olive oil

3 zucchini (courgettes) – sliced and then diced into small pieces

1 zucchini (courgette) – thinly sliced

1 teaspoon salt and black pepper

8 eggs

THE KEY

YOU CAN TELL THAT THE MOUSSE IS READY WHEN A KNIFE INSERTED INTO THE CENTER OF THE MOUSSE COMES OUT CLEAN.

1 Preheat oven to 400 degrees.

2 Pour a little olive oil into a medium-sized pan, and sauté the diced zucchini until soft and browned – approximately 10 minutes.

3 In a blender, purée the diced zucchini with the salt and pepper. Add the eggs to the purée and purée again until well blended.

4 In the same pan, sauté the zucchini slices until soft and lightly browned. Set aside.

5 Oil eight individual 4-inch ramekins. Place one slice of the sautéed zucchini on the bottom of the ramekin. Place five zucchini slices around the side of the ramekin – they will stick to the sides with the oil.

6 Pour the zucchini purée into the ramekin until it is almost 2/3 full.

7 Place the ramekins in a deep baking dish that is large enough to hold all of them and carefully pour hot water around the ramekins so that the water comes half way up the sides.

8 Bake in the oven for 35-40 minutes until the mousse has set.

9 Spoon a little salsa di pomodoro into the center of each warm plate. Unmould the mousse by running a knife around the inside of the ramekin and then inverting it onto the sauce.

Origins

Zucchini are from the squash family but, surprisingly, only became popular in the 20th century. In America, they are known as zucchini from the Italian name as they were imported by Italian immigrants. The English, on the other hand, refer to this vegetable as a courgette, as they became aware of them through French cooking and, in large part, due to the writings of Elizabeth David.

Salsa di Pomodoro

Olive oil

1 small onion – chopped

1 shallot – finely chopped

1 lb ripe tomatoes – peeled, seeded and diced

2 tablespoons fresh parsley – finely chopped

1 sprig fresh thyme

1 bay leaf

Fresh black pepper

Salt

1/4 cup fresh basil – finely chopped

1   Heat 1 tablespoon of olive oil in a small skillet, place over medium heat and cook the onion and shallot until very soft, about 10-12 minutes. Add the diced tomatoes, thyme, bay leaf, parsley, salt and pepper. Bring to a boil, reduce heat and simmer until very thick – about 45 minutes to 1 hour.

2   Remove the thyme and bay leaf. Add the reserved basil to the sauce just before serving, stirring well to combine.

Preparing fish with William, Ann Marie's son.

GRILLED FISH IN GRAPE LEAVES WITH A DILL BUTTER SAUCE

Across the Mediterranean, we have found many variations of dishes with vine leaves, each country having specialties of fish, meat, rice, or a combination thereof being wrapped in vine leaves; the dolmades of Greece and Turkey are the prime example. The leaves impart a slightly sweet aromatic flavor to the contents when grilling fish this way, as the fish steams inside the wrapping but also takes up some of the smoky flavor from the grill.

Serves 8 people

4 medium-sized whole fish such as trout, striped bass, small pink salmon, etc., gutted and scaled but tail and head left on. *Alternatively, you can use thick slices of filleted fish such as halibut or sea bass; if you use the filleted fish you will need a 6 oz slice per person*

3 tablespoons olive oil

Salt and pepper

Juice of 2 lemons

Lots of grape leaves (or, if unavailable, you can use fig leaves) – wash the leaves but do not dry them

THE KEY

TRY TO COVER UP ALL OF THE FISH WITH THE VINE LEAVES. THEY ACT AS A SEAL, KEEPING MOISTURE IN THE FISH AS IT COOKS.

1   Pour the olive oil into a small bowl and add the salt and pepper and the lemon juice. Using a fork or small whisk, mix the ingredients well. Spoon a little of the olive oil mixture on each of the whole fish, including inside the cavity or, if using fillets, on both sides.

2   Carefully wrap the fish up with the grape leaves or fig leaves and secure them with cooking twine that has been previously soaked in water or with skewers that have also been soaked (they burn if you don't soak them). If you have a fish grill, place the pieces of wrapped fish inside and place over the grill about 4 inches above the coals. Grill for 4-5 minutes on each side. Serve the fish still wrapped in its package.

Dill Butter Sauce

4 oz (1 stick) butter

3 shallots – finely sliced

1 small bunch dill – finely chopped

Juice of 1/2 lemon

1   Melt the butter in a small saucepan and cook the shallots until golden but not too browned. Add all the dill at the last moment and then stir in the lemon juice. Spoon this over the hot grilled fish.

Timbales of Rice with Fresh Herbs

Serves 8 people

2 cups basmati rice

3 1/4 cups water

Fresh dill – finely chopped

Fresh parsley – finely chopped

Fresh chives – finely chopped

2 tablespoons butter

Salt and pepper

1 Rinse the basmati rice under cold water until the water runs clear. Place the cleaned rice in a saucepan and add the water. Bring to a boil. Once boiling, reduce to a simmer and cover. Cook per the instructions on the packet, or if cooking in a rice cooker, cook per the manufacturer's instructions.

2 Place the cooked rice in a large bowl with all the chopped herbs and the butter. Mix until well combined. Check the seasoning and add salt and pepper as needed. Using a small oiled ramekin or stainless ring, fill it with the rice mixture and invert it onto each serving plate.

Origins

Timbales used to mean a type of drinking goblet. Silver christening cups are a form of timbales. In cooking, the term refers to a type of mould in which all manner of foods are prepared, usually pastry- lined, but it can also refer to the shape of the moulded foods, as in this dish.

Olivia and Alexandre Groom helping in the kitchen.

Origins

Crème in French means not just cream but is also a cooking term. As there is no word in the French language to mean custard, crème is used. Crème Anglaise literally means 'English cream,' and as it sounds nicer than custard, it is widely used in restaurants and cookbooks in English-speaking countries

PEACH TART AND LAVENDER CRÈME ANGLAISE

Serves 8 people

Peach Tart

Use the short crust pastry recipe on page 26 and proceed to the point where you will refrigerate the dough

4 lbs firm ripe peaches (you can use yellow or white varieties or a combination of both)

2 oz (1/2 stick) butter

1 tablespoon light brown sugar

2 tablespoons apricot jam

1   Preheat the oven to 400 degrees.

2   Remove the dough from the fridge. On a lightly floured board, roll out the dough in an even manner to an inch larger than the size of your mould. Butter the tart mould and then line the mould with the dough. Trim the edges with a sharp knife and then prick the dough in the bottom of the tart pan with the tines of a fork.

3   Line the dough with a piece of foil, shiny side down, and fill the tart with pie weights – if you do not have pie weights you can use dried beans. Bake the tart for 15 minutes until it is just golden. Remove from the oven and set aside after you have removed the foil and pie weights.

4   Whilst the tart shell is cooking, prepare the peaches. Cut them, unpeeled, into quarters, or if they are very large, into eighths. Set aside.

5   Melt the butter in a large skillet over high heat. When the butter is foaming, add the brown sugar and cook for 1 minute. Add the peach slices to the butter mixture and toss to coat well. Remove from the heat.

6   Brush the partially cooked tart shell with the apricot jam and then start placing the peach slices, cut side up around the edge of the dough, working your way in concentric circles to the middle of the tart. The peaches will form a pattern that looks like an open flower.

7   Return the tart to the oven and bake for a further 6-7 minutes. The shell should be a golden brown color. Remove and let cool to room temperature. Serve with the Lavender Crème Anglaise.

Origins

Peaches originated in China in the 5th century BC and came to Europe through Persia via Alexander the Great.
The word peach comes from pêche in French, which comes from the Latin, Perscium Malum. During the reign of Louis XIV,
certain varieties of peach were known by the nickname, *les tetons de venus* –Venus breasts.

Lavender Crème Anglaise

1 cup milk

2 egg yolks

3 oz (1/2 cup) sugar

3 stems of lavender – very finely chopped

1/2 teaspoon vanilla extract

1 In a small saucepan, bring the milk to a boil and then immediately remove from heat.

2 In a heat-proof bowl, beat the egg yolks with a whisk until pale, then add the sugar and beat again. Pour the hot milk slowly over the egg yolks, stirring constantly. Place the bowl over a saucepan of simmering water. Add in the lavender and cook gently without boiling until the mixture thickens and coats the back of a spoon.

3 Remove from the heat and add the vanilla and beat slightly. Strain the mixture and set aside to cool. It should have the consistency of a thickish cream and should be easy to pour.

Tomates Mimosas
Provençal Rack of Lamb with a Gâteau de Crêpes au Gruyére
Haricots Verts a l'Ail
Orange Crème Caramel

COOKING SCHEDULE

Starting 2 hours before you plan to eat your first course

- Make the orange crème caramel.

- Prepare the rack of lamb and set aside for 30 minutes before cooking.

- Prepare the gâteau de crêpes (the gâteau de crêpes can be made earlier in the day through step 4 and then refrigerated).

- Prepare and cook the garlic for the haricots verts – it takes 45 minutes.

- Prepare and cook tomatoes for the tomates mimosa.

- Put the gâteau de crêpes in the oven 30 minutes before you plan to eat the main course.

- Cook the haricots verts and finish the dish.

- Start cooking the rack of lamb about 15 minutes before you sit down to the first course.

- Finish and serve the tomates mimosa.

TOMATES MIMOSAS

Geneviève Fay was my wonderful French grandmother. She gave me a passion for 'L'art de la table.' Cooking with her, as I grew up, was a special treat. As a little girl, this is one of the first things I learned to make with her, and I was always enchanted by the tale that accompanied it… the tomatoes are covered with a mixture which, she said, resembled mimosa. A mysterious lady who had given her the recipe, told her that she was reminded of the mimosa she had seen in Japan and, in fact, called them 'Tomates Japonaise' or Japanese Tomatoes. I never found out who the lady was but the recipe lives on.

—PASCALE

Serves 8

Olive oil

2 cloves of garlic – mashed

16 small or 8 medium-sized ripe, yet firm, tomatoes – each cut in half

Salt and pepper

3 eggs – hardboiled and peeled

4-5 tablespoons crème fraiche

Chives – finely chopped

Parsley – finely chopped

Basil – very finely sliced

1   In a heavy-bottomed ovenproof pan, heat a little olive oil adding the garlic and the tomato halves placed face down. Cook for 4-5 minutes over medium heat, so that the tomatoes are sizzling and beginning to change color. They should be a little browned. Turn the tomatoes over and continue to cook for another 5-7 minutes. Add a little salt and pepper half-way through. When the tomatoes are cooked but still holding their shape turn off the heat, leaving the tomatoes in the dish.

2   Whilst the tomatoes are cooking, prepare the eggs. In a medium-sized bowl, mash the eggs with a fork or potato masher. Stir in the crème fraiche, the chives, parsley and basil. The mixture should look quite green from the herbs. Add some black pepper, a pinch of salt and set aside.

3   Just before serving the dish, spoon a heaped teaspoon (in the case of the small tomatoes) or a tablespoon (in the case of the medium tomatoes) of the egg mixture on top of each tomato half. Place the baking dish under the grill (broiler) until the egg mixture is golden brown. Serve these hot.

Geneviève Fay – 'Mamie' in her kitchen. Briançon, France 1992

Origins

Tomatoes originated in Peru and were called *tomatl*. They were imported by Spain in the
16th century and were spread throughout Europe from there. In certain countries they have more amorous names;

PROVENÇAL RACK OF LAMB WITH GÂTEAU DE CRÊPES AU GRUYÉRE

Serves 8 people

2 racks of lamb

4 cloves garlic – crushed

1 1/2 tablespoons coarse salt

1 tablespoon freshly ground black pepper

1/4 cup olive oil

1/4 cup fresh rosemary – chopped

1/4 cup fresh thyme – chopped

1 tablespoon oregano– chopped

THE KEY

LETTING THE MEAT REST (ANY MEAT IN FACT) FOR AT LEAST 10 MINUTES WILL ALLOW THE MEAT'S NATURAL JUICES TO RETURN TO THE EXTREMITIES OF THE ROAST. THE INTERNAL TEMPERATURE OF THE MEAT WILL NOT DIMINISH AS IT RESTS. IF YOU SLICE A ROAST AS SOON AS IT COMES OUT OF THE OVEN, WITHOUT LETTING IT REST, ALL THE JUICE WILL RUN OUT ONTO THE CUTTING BOARD, MAKING THE MEAT MUCH LESS TENDER AND JUICY.

1 With a sharp knife, score the back of the rack of lamb in a criss-cross pattern, cutting 1/2 inch through to the meat.

2 In a small bowl mix all the remaining ingredients so that they create a thick paste. Spoon the paste over the racks of lamb, rubbing it thoroughly into the skin and into the cuts (you can leave the lamb like this for 30 minutes before hand, as the flavors will permeate the meat).

3 Preheat the oven to 400 degrees.

4 Pour the olive oil into an oven-proof skillet and heat over medium heat. Sauté the racks in the skillet for 5 minutes on each side, then place the skillet in the oven and roast for a further 15 minutes for pink meat. Remove from the oven and place the racks on a wooden chopping board and cover them loosely with foil – let them rest for 10 minutes before cutting.

5 Place the skillet back on the stove top and de-glaze the skillet with a little red wine, reducing the pan juices by half. Cut the racks and place two chops onto each plate and pour a little of the pan juices over the racks.

GÂTEAU DE CRÊPES AU GRUYÉRE

This sumptuous and quite decadent dish is a creation of my aunt Marie-France and uncle Yves Delas, who, like my grandmother, are excellent cooks. Their food is rich and plentiful and the atmosphere in their kitchen warm and inviting. Preparations for the evening meal will always begin with a glass of wine for the cooks, accompanied by a little homemade saucisson or a little local goat cheese. Meals in the Delas household are always lively, with conversation often revolving around food, but I have yet to find out the origin of this gâteau which they say is a secret.

—PASCALE

Origins

Crêpes are a type of pancake that are very, very thin and whose batter is poured into a flat, almost rimless pan and cooked on both sides. The word crêpe comes from the Latin 'crispus,' meaning wavy or curly.

Serves 8-10 people

For the crêpe batter:

9 oz (2 cups) unbleached flour

1/2 teaspoon salt

2 cups milk

1/2 cup water

6 eggs – beaten together in a small bowl

3 oz (3/4 stick) butter – melted

For the filling:

10 oz Gruyére cheese – grated (3 cups)

8 oz crème fraiche

Salt and pepper

1   Put the dry ingredients in the bowl of a standing mixer (or in a large bowl if you are whisking this by hand). With the mixer running, pour in the milk, water, melted butter and eggs. Keep whisking until the batter is smooth.

2   Heat a small frying pan (or crêpe pan if you have one) or small skillet – they should all be about 7 inches in diameter so that the pan is very hot. Pour a little oil onto a paper towel and wipe the surface of the pan with the paper towel. Pour about 1/3 cup of the batter into the pan and then tilt the pan so that the batter covers the entire surface. Cook the crêpe until golden brown and then flip it over, cooking a minute more. (You may lose the first one or two as they might stick or not form properly – don't worry this is normal).

3   Preheat the oven to 350 degrees.

4   When the crêpe is cooked, place it in a round ovenproof dish. Spoon a little of the crème fraiche over the crêpe and then sprinkle some of the Gruyére cheese over that. Add a pinch of salt and one or two turns on a pepper mill. Repeat with each crêpe until the batter is finished *(about 20-24 crêpes – that is not a typo!)*. You can make it, up to this point, a couple of hours ahead of time. Just cover the dish with plastic wrap and refrigerate until ready to bake.

5   When the gâteau is finished, place it in the oven and cook for 20-25 minutes. Remove from the oven and wait 5 minutes before cutting the gâteau into pie shaped slices, as this makes it easier to serve.

HARICOTS VERTS A L'AIL

Serves 8 people

1 head of garlic

Olive oil

1 1/2 lbs haricots verts

Salt

1 oz butter

1 small bunch parsley – finely chopped

1   Preheat the oven to 350 degrees.

2   Chop off the top quarter of the garlic head and drizzle a little olive oil onto the garlic. Replace the top of the garlic head and wrap the entire head in foil. Bake in a preheated oven at 350 degrees for 45 minutes.

3   Bring a large saucepan of salted water to a boil and cook the haricots verts until they are just cooked (about 6 minutes if you like them al denté). Drain the haricots verts, and then return them to the saucepan. Remove the garlic from the foil and squish out the softened roasted garlic into the haricots verts. Add the butter and parsley and toss to coat evenly.

ORANGE CRÈME CARAMEL

I stopped at my grandma Nonni's house every day on the way home from school. As she always had plenty of eggs, cream and milk on hand from the family farm, we would always get a special sweet treat. Sometimes cookies and milk, or rice pudding, and sometimes she would make a great traditional crème caramel, although we always called it custard. We would sit around the dining room table eating this simple good food, learning how to play pinochle, bridge and gin rummy! This version was inspired by the memory of all those visits and by a huge basket of oranges that arrived on my doorstep one morning.

—ANN MARIE

Serves 8 people

For the caramel:

5 oz (3/4 cup) sugar

3 tablespoons water

1   Blend the sugar and water together in a saucepan and bring to a simmer. Be sure that the sugar has dissolved completely. The liquid should be completely clear.

2   Cover the pan tightly and boil the syrup for several minutes over moderately high heat – keep checking the mixture and boil until the bubbles are thick. Uncover the pan and continue boiling. The color of the syrup will change quickly from white to a light brown caramel. When it reaches this stage continue boiling a few seconds more and then remove from the heat as it will continue to darken. You can put the bottom of the pan in some cold water to stop the cooking process at this point.

3   Pour the caramel into the bottom of the ramekins and swirl them around so that the entire bottom and part of the sides are covered with the caramel. Please be very careful as the caramel is extremely hot. Use all the caramel, distributing it evenly amongst the ramekins. Set aside.

For the crème:

3 oz (1/2 cup) sugar

3 large eggs

3 egg yolks

2 1/4 cups milk

1/4 cup orange juice and the zest of 3 oranges

1   Preheat the oven to 350 degrees.

2   In a medium-sized saucepan heat the milk with the orange juice and orange zests, until hot. Remove from the heat and set aside.

3   To make the crème: blend the whole eggs, egg yolks and sugar in a medium-sized bowl. Stir the ingredients together rather than beating them to minimize foam.

4   Gradually pour the milk into the egg mixture while stirring, as opposed to beating, again to minimize any bubbles or foam. Pour the mixture through a strainer before filling the ramekins.

5   Divide the liquid evenly amongst the ramekins and then set the ramekins into a baking pan. Pour boiling water around the ramekins so that the water comes half-way up the sides.

Origins

In Italy, Spain and France, there is a wide use of crème type desserts, often called flan, from the old French word *flaon* which, in turn, came from the Latin *flado* meaning custard. In Middle English it was called flathon, then flawn and now flan.

6   Bake for 30-35 minutes. The crème is ready when a sharp knife inserted 1/4 inch from the edge comes out clean. The center may tremble slightly.

7   When the crème caramels are ready, remove from the oven and let them rest in their ramekins until you are ready to serve them. You can make this dish the day before and keep the finished crèmes in the fridge. To serve, run a sharp knife around the edge of the ramekin and then place a small plate over the ramekin. Invert the two. The crème caramel will slowly slip out, with the caramel pouring over the top.

THE KEY

DO NOT STIR THE CARAMEL MIXTURE, AS THIS WILL CAUSE IT TO CRYSTALLIZE. MAKE SURE YOU STRAIN THE CRÈME BEFORE PUTTING IT INTO THE RAMEKINS. YOU WILL HAVE A *MUCH* SMOOTHER DESSERT AS A RESULT. CHECK THE WATER IN THE BAKING DISH — IT MUST NOT BOIL AS THIS WILL CAUSE THE CUSTARD TO BECOME GRAINY, BUT THE WATER MUST BE ALMOST SIMMERING, OTHERWISE THE CUSTARD WILL TAKE AGES TO COOK. IF THE WATER IS TOO HOT JUST ADD A LITTLE COLD WATER TO REGULATE THE TEMPERATURE.

Italian Spring Salad

Ravioli Gigante ai Funghi with a Sage and Butter Sauce

Lavender Pots de Crème with Lemon Thyme Meringues

COOKING SCHEDULE

Earlier in the day

- Make the pots de crème as they need at least 2-3 hours to set.
- It is easier to make the meringues earlier as well, as they need 90 minutes to cook.

Starting 2 hours before you plan to eat your first course

- Make the pasta dough 30 minutes before preparing the ravioli.
- Prepare the sauce for the ravioli.
- Make the ravioli stuffing and form the ravioli.
- Make the Italian spring salad.
- Cook the ravioli between first and second courses.

ITALIAN SPRING SALAD

Serves 8 people

1/3 cup extra virgin olive oil

3 tablespoons balsamic vinegar

Salt and pepper

1 lb baby arugula

1/2 lb mixed salad greens

1/3 English cucumber – peeled, seeded and diced

6 large, ripe tomatoes – diced

2 heads radicchio – leaves cleaned but left intact

1   Pour the olive oil, balsamic vinegar and some salt and pepper into the bottom of a large bowl and whisk well to combine. Place the serving utensils over the top of the vinaigrette and then place the arugula, mixed greens, cucumber and tomatoes on top of the utensils.

2   When you are ready to serve the salad, remove the serving utensils so that the greens fall into the vinaigrette and then toss well. Place one or two radicchio leaves on each person's plate and then fill the leaves with the salad mixture. This is delicious served with a warm ciabatta or olive bread.

Ann Marie's daughter, Emily, learning the fine art of making ravioli.

RAVIOLI GIGANTE AI FUNGHI WITH A SAGE AND BUTTER SAUCE

I have always had a love for ravioli and their cousins agnolotti, but when I met Ann Marie I found out that they are truly an affair of the heart and an affirmation of the old adage — a way to a man's heart is through his stomach.

—PASCALE

It's true — I admit that I seduced my husband by making him, on our second date, handmade ravioli, stuffed with veal and Parmesan. He watched me making them for an hour, as he now says; after that he knew I was the woman he was going to marry…that was 20 years ago.

—ANN MARIE

Serves 8 – makes 16 four-inch raviolis

For the dough:

12 oz (2 1/2 cups) flour

3 1/2 oz (1/2 cup) semolina flour

3 extra large eggs

1 teaspoon of salt

1   Place the flours in a mound on a large flat surface. If you can, work on marble as the dough sticks less to the surface.

2   Make a fist and place it in the center of the mound, creating a well. Place the eggs and salt in the well. With a fork gently beat the eggs together, incorporating the flour a little at a time until the mixture forms a gooey, lumpy mass. Using your hands, continue kneading the dough, adding a bit more flour, if necessary, if the dough is too wet, until it is completely smooth.

3   Now that your dough is smooth and elastic, cut the dough into four pieces and shape it into disks, as it will be easier to work with that way. Wrap the dough in plastic wrap and let it rest for 30 minutes.

4   Flour a rolling pin and your work surface and begin rolling out the dough until it is 1/8 inch in thickness. Repeat with the remaining dough. If you have a pasta machine, start on the widest setting and repeatedly feed the dough through until you are on the second to last setting.

For the filling:

4 tablespoons olive oil

2 tablespoons butter

1 large onion – peeled and finely chopped

8 oz Portobello mushrooms – finely chopped (this is about three 4-inch mushrooms)

2 oz dried Porcini mushrooms which have been rehydrated – finely chopped (you should have 3 cups)

3 oz (2 cups) Parmesan cheese – freshly grated

Salt and pepper to taste

1   Put the olive oil and butter in a large pan over medium heat. Add the onion and sauté until soft. Then add the mushrooms, cooking them until soft and the excess liquid has evaporated. The mushrooms should be almost dry.

2   Remove from the pan and put the mixture into a mixing bowl. Add the Parmesan, salt and pepper to taste. Combine well.

To assemble and cook the ravioli:

1 Lay out 2 sheets of the finished dough on a lightly floured surface. Drop tablespoonsful of the filling about 4 inches apart on each sheet of the dough. You should have 2 rows of 4 mounds per sheet. Dip your fingers in a small bowl of water and lightly wet the dough that surrounds the mounds of stuffing. Cover with the remaining sheets of dough.

2 With your fingers, gently press around the mounds of stuffing, taking care not to tear the dough or to leave pockets of air. With a knife or a very sharp pizza cutter, cut the ravioli. Be sure that the edges of the ravioli are firmly closed or the stuffing will come out during cooking.

3 Bring a large pot of water to a rapid boil. Place a few ravioli at a time in the pot, and cook until they float to the surface of the water, they will be al dente at this point. Take one out of the pot and let it cool and taste it to see if you like the texture. If you like the ravioli softer, cook them for another 2 minutes.

Sage and butter sauce

6 oz (1 1/2 sticks) butter

10 large fresh sage leaves – torn into thirds

1 In a small saucepan melt the butter with the sage leaves. Let the butter foam a little and become a little brown. This gives a slight nutty flavor to the butter, but be careful not to over cook it, as it will taste burnt and bitter if left too long. Remove from the heat and spoon over the ravioli.

This is a labor of love but well worth the effort. —ANN MARIE

THE KEY
MAKE SURE YOUR DOUGH IS NOT TOO THIN AND THAT THE RAVIOLI ARE WELL SEALED OR THE FILLING WILL COME OUT DURING THE COOKING PROCESS.

Origins

It is assumed by most people that ravioli are Italian in origin, but the earliest known appearance of these lovely stuffed pastas are in medieval Provençe, where they were known as *rauioles*. This underscores again the close link between the cuisines of the French and Italian Riviera, and how certain dishes, such as ravioli appear, albeit in a slightly different form, in different cultures around the world – they are known, for example, as *mantou and jiozi* in China, *momo* in Tibet, *manti* in Turkey or *pel'meni*, which is a form of Russian wonton.

LAVENDER POTS DE CRÈME WITH LEMON THYME MERINGUES

Lavender Pots de Crème

Serves 8 people

2 1/2 cups cream

6 sprigs lavender – coarsely chopped

5 1/2 oz super fine sugar

Just under 1/3 cup lemon juice

1/3 cup lavender flowers – coarsely chopped

1   Combine the cream, chopped sprigs of lavender and sugar in a medium-sized saucepan placed over medium heat and bring the cream to a boil, then immediately reduce to a simmer and cook for 5-6 minutes. Remove the pan from the heat, stir in the lemon juice and let the mixture cool down for about 10 minutes.

2   Strain the cream through a fine mesh sieve into a bowl, discarding the solids. Stir in the chopped lavender flowers.

3   Divide the cream evenly amongst 8 small cups or ramekins, cover and refrigerate for 3 hours or until the mixture has set. Serve with the lemon thyme meringues.

THE KEY
LIKE THE CRÈME CARAMEL, IT IS ESSENTIAL TO STRAIN THE CREAM MIXTURE AS THIS WILL GIVE A FINE TEXTURE TO THE POTS DE CRÈME.

Lemon Thyme Meringues

Serves 8-10 people

3 egg whites

7 1/2 oz (1 cup plus 2 tablespoons) sugar – try to use the super fine sugar

2 tablespoons lemon thyme – finely chopped (if you cannot find lemon thyme, use regular thyme plus the zest of one more lemon)

Zest of 1 lemon – finely chopped

1   Preheat the oven to 225 degrees.

2   Place the egg whites in the bowl of a standing mixer and beat until they hold soft peaks. Gradually add the sugar, a tablespoon at a time and whisk until the whites are stiff and very glossy. Add in the chopped thyme and lemon zest and beat a few seconds more so that it is evenly distributed in the meringue mixture.

3   Place large tablespoonsful of the meringue mixture onto a parchment lined baking sheet, leaving at least 1 inch between them. You will need 2 baking sheets for this recipe. Bake in the oven for 1 1/2 hours or until they are dry. They should not turn golden, but rather should be a pale cream color when finished.

THE KEY
TO HAVE BEAUTIFUL FIRM MERINGUES, MAKE SURE THAT YOU ADD THE SUGAR ONLY AFTER THE EGG WHITES HOLD SOFT PEAKS. IF YOU ADD THE SUGAR TOO SOON, THE MERINGUES WILL NOT HOLD THEIR SHAPE AS WELL.

Mache Salad with Goat Cheese, Prosciutto and Pistachios
Roasted Beef Tenderloin with a Lavender Herb Crust and a
Red Wine Sauce
A Medley of Spring Peas
Mango Soup with Gingered Raspberries

COOKING SCHEDULE

This can be done as much as 6 hours ahead of time

- Prepare the mango soup and refrigerate in individual bowls.

Starting 2 hours before eating your first course

- Prepare the ingredients for the gingered raspberries and set aside.
- Make the red wine sauce that goes with the beef tenderloin.
- Prepare the beef tenderloin.
- Make the mache salad.
- Place the beef tenderloin in the oven about 25 minutes before you sit down to eat the first course – it will cook whilst you're eating and can rest between the two courses.
- After the main course, finish preparing the raspberries. They take just a few minutes.

MACHE SALAD WITH GOAT CHEESE, PROSCIUTTO AND PISTACHIOS

We had been recipe testing desserts for hours when Pascale said she needed food. I opened the fridge door and found only mache, prosciutto, goat cheese and pistachios, with which I made this salad. It was an instant favorite!

— ANN MARIE

Serves 8 people

3 tablespoons olive oil

1 tablespoon apple cider vinegar or Jerez vinegar

Salt and pepper

8 oz mache (also known as lamb's lettuce)

8 slices of prosciutto – cut into thin strips

6 oz goat cheese – crumbled into pieces *(for a truly extravagant version use the goat cheese that has truffles in it)*

2 oz (1/2 cup) pistachios – roughly chopped

1 In the bottom of a large salad bowl, combine the olive oil, vinegar, a good pinch of salt and two or three turns of a pepper grinder. Whisk well to emulsify. Place your salad utensils over the top of the vinaigrette.

2 Place the mache on top of the utensils, along with the strips of prosciutto, goat cheese and pistachios. When you are ready to serve the salad, remove the utensils so that the greens fall into the vinaigrette and toss so that all the ingredients are well coated. Serve with warm bread.

ROASTED BEEF TENDERLOIN WITH A LAVENDER HERB CRUST AND A RED WINE SAUCE

This is an adapted version of a dish which dates from my catering days. The success of this colorful dish inspired the creation of a special dried herb mix for our new product line.   —ANN MARIE

Serves 8 people

A 4 lb beef tenderloin

Olive oil

Medium coarse salt

Freshly ground black pepper

6 tablespoons fresh lavender, rosemary and thyme – roughly chopped

1 oz (1/4 cup) pink peppercorns – crushed

1   Preheat oven to 400 degrees.

2   Cover the tenderloin with olive oil and then sprinkle a large pinch of salt and pepper over the meat.

3   In a small bowl combine the fresh herbs and the pink peppercorns. Cover the tenderloin with all of the herbs pressing them in gently to adhere to the oil. Pour 2 tablespoons of olive oil into a roasting pan and place the tenderloin in the pan.

4   Roast for 40-45 minutes for medium-rare meat. The internal temperature should be 125 degrees.

5   Remove the meat from the oven and let it rest, covered loosely with foil for 10 minutes before slicing. Serve with the red wine sauce.

Red Wine Sauce

1 tablespoon olive oil

2 oz shallots and garlic – minced

4 cloves garlic – minced

1 carrot – diced

3 cups red wine

1 1/2 quarts beef stock (see page 67)

8 oz pearl onions – blanched for 1 minute and then peeled

8 oz Crimini mushrooms – quartered

3 oz (3/4 stick) butter

Salt and pepper to taste

1   Pour the olive oil into a small sauté pan over medium-high heat and add the shallots, garlic and carrots and cook until caramelized.

2   Add the red wine and cook until the volume has reduced by half.

3   Add the beef stock and reduce by 25%. Strain the liquid and reserve.

4   In a separate pan, heat a little more olive oil and cook the pearl onions until golden brown. Add the mushrooms and cook for just 3 minutes until just softened. Add the red wine liquid and keep the sauce warm. Just before serving, add the butter to the sauce a little at a time. This will give the sauce a wonderful sheen, but be careful not to let the sauce boil as this will cause the butter to separate.

A MEDLEY OF SPRING PEAS

Serves 8 people

Olive oil

2 shallots – finely chopped

2 green onions – finely sliced

1 1/2 lbs spring peas – use the smallest, freshest peas you can find (you can also use a mixture of different varieties if you like – as long as they are uniform in size)

1 small bunch chives – finely chopped

1/2 cup chicken broth (see page 66)

Salt and pepper

1   Pour a little olive oil into a large sauté pan placed over medium heat. Add the shallots and green onions and cook for 3 minutes. Add in the spring peas and chives and cook for 3 minutes more.

2   Add in the chicken broth, a good pinch of salt and some pepper and let simmer for 2 minutes. Serve alongside the sliced beef tenderloin.

THE KEY

CHOOSING FRESH PEAS IS ESSENTIAL. THEIR SKINS SHOULD BE BRIGHT GREEN, SHINY AND SQUEAK SLIGHTLY WHEN RUBBED TOGETHER. AVOID PEAS THAT HAVE LIGHT GREEN OR YELLOW SKINS AS THEY WILL NOT TASTE SWEET AND FRESH. YOU CAN MIX SNAP PEAS, OR YOUNG FAVA BEANS INTO THIS RAGOUT IF YOU LIKE. REMEMBER THAT THE FAVA BEANS WILL NEED TO BE PEELED.

MANGO SOUP WITH GINGERED RASPBERRIES

I made this soup for my birthday, which we celebrated in Ann Marie and Scott's lovely home. We had been on a ginger craze for weeks when mangoes presented themselves. It had been unusually hot that spring and a chilled soup seemed to be the perfect thing. The combination of the raspberries with the ginger was an extra treat on top of the mangoes.

—PASCALE

Serves 8 people — This will make enough for a small bowl per person

3 ripe mangoes – peeled and the flesh cut into pieces

Juice of 6 oranges

2 oz (1/2 stick) butter

1 1/4 oz (3 tablespoons) brown sugar

1 tablespoon ginger – freshly grated

2 oz (4 tablespoons) crystallized ginger – chopped

Zest of 1 1/2 lemons

2 baskets raspberries

1 Place all the mango pieces in a food processor and pulse until you have a thick purée. Then, with the motor running, add the orange juice in a gradual stream. You will end up with a smooth soup that will be quite thick. Pour the soup into individual bowls and refrigerate until serving time.

2 Melt the butter in a pan that is large enough to hold all the raspberries. When the butter is bubbling, add the brown sugar and cook for 2 minutes. Add in the fresh and crystallized ginger and the lemon zest and cook for a further 2-3 minutes. Set aside.

3 Just before serving the soup, reheat the sugar-ginger mixture, add the raspberries to the mixture and cook for 30 seconds over high heat, so the raspberries are coated with the ginger mixture and they just begin to release their juices. Remove from the heat and spoon one large spoonful into the center of each bowl of soup. Serve at once to keep the contrast between the cold soup and the warm raspberries.

Mango trees originated in India and Malaysia in about 2000 BC. The word mango comes from the Tamil *man-kay* or *man-gay*. It made its way around the world in the 18th and 19th centuries, reaching the West Indies, then Florida and Hawaii. Their local cuisines showcase this fruit in their salsas, chutneys and relishs and have become synonymous with these parts of the world.

Ginger is a plant of South Eastern Asian origin. It is cultivated for its rhizomes or underground roots and is greatly used in Eastern cuisines. Its use was widespread in Europe, especially in England during the Middle Ages, a vestige of which is now found in British puddings, pastries and biscuits, e.g., ginger breads, ginger tea biscuits and the like. Its use is more widespread with the fusion of regional foods.

TAKING STOCK

We are often asked why we take the time to make our own stocks. The answer is simple; they just taste so much better than those you can buy commercially. A lot of people lament the time it takes to make stock, but once you have tasted a homemade one, we think you will agree that it is well worth the effort.

Chicken Stock

Makes 2 quarts

2-3 lbs chicken parts, e.g., legs or backs

2 stalks of celery – roughly chopped

3 carrots – peeled and roughly chopped

2 large onions – quartered with peel intact

4 cloves garlic – peeled

2 teaspoons salt

A couple of turns of fresh pepper

3 quarts of cold water

1   Preheat the oven to 375 degrees.

2   On a baking sheet, place the chicken parts, celery, carrots, onions, garlic and season with salt and pepper. Roast for 1 hour.

3   Remove the roasting pan from the oven and carefully place the roasted chicken and vegetables in a stockpot with 3 quarts of cold water.

4   Place the roasting pan on top of the stove over medium-high heat. Pour in 1 cup water and scrape all the brown bits of vegetables, etc., off the bottom of the pan. There is lots of flavor left in the bottom of the pan in the caramelized bits and pieces, so take advantage of it. Pour the liquid from the roasting pan into the stockpot with the chicken and vegetables. Simmer for 2 hours. During that time, remove the scum (a gray looking foam) that comes to the surface of the stock, carefully, with a large spoon. It is very important to do this regularly during the first 45 minutes of cooking to keep a good clean flavor in your stock.

5   After 2 hours, remove from the heat, let cool and strain the stock. When you are straining the stock, do so carefully, avoiding pressing down and squashing the meat and vegetables in the strainer. Your patience in letting the stock filter naturally through the strainer will be well rewarded with a good, clear, fresh tasting stock.

6   The stock will keep in the fridge for 3 days. You can, of course, freeze the stock, which we recommend doing in different-sized containers for ease of use. *If you are using glass mason jars to freeze your stock, make sure you leave at LEAST 1 1/2 inches of space between the top of the stock and the lid, as the stock expands as it freezes. If you overfill the jar, it will crack in the freezer.*

KEY

HERE ARE A FEW KEY TIPS TO MAKING A GOOD CLEAR STOCK.

ALWAYS ADD COLD WATER TO THE MEAT AND VEGETABLES AS ADDING HOT WATER WILL CAUSE THE MEAT TO RELEASE PROTEINS THAT WILL CAUSE THE STOCK TO BECOME CLOUDY. SIMILARLY, DO NOT BOIL YOUR STOCK OR THIS WILL CAUSE THE SAME REACTION. WHEN THE STOCK IS COOKING, RESIST THE TEMPTATION TO STIR ALL THE INGREDIENTS TOGETHER. THIS WILL CAUSE THE SAME PROBLEM; JUST LET THE STOCK COOK WITHOUT DISTURBING IT.

DON'T BE TEMPTED TO ADD MORE WATER TO GET MORE STOCK. THE STOCK WILL BE MORE FLAVORFUL WITH THE AMOUNTS INDICATED. IF YOU WANT TO MAKE MORE, DOUBLE ALL THE INGREDIENTS.

Beef Stock

Makes 2 quarts

3 to 4 lbs of beef bones

2 carrots – peeled and cut into 1-inch pieces

2 celery stalks – cut into 1-inch pieces

4 cloves garlic – peeled

1 large onion – quartered with skins on

1 bay leaf

4 sprigs thyme

Salt and pepper to taste

4 quarts cold water

1   Preheat the oven to 350 degrees.

2   Place the beef bones, carrots, celery, garlic and onion in a roasting pan and roast for 1 hour.

3   Remove the roasting pan from the oven and carefully place the roasted beef bones and vegetables in a stockpot with 4 quarts of water. Add in the bay leaf and thyme, salt and pepper.

4   Place the now empty roasting pan on top of the stove over medium-high heat. Pour in 1 cup of water and scrape all the brown bits of vegetables, etc., off the bottom of the pan. Pour the liquid from the roasting pan into the stockpot with the beef bones and vegetables. Slowly bring to a simmer and cook for 4 hours. During that time, remove the scum (a gray looking foam) that comes to the surface of the stock, carefully, with a large spoon. It is very important to do this regularly during the first hour of cooking to keep a good clean flavor in your stock. If the amount of liquid reduces too much, add in a little more cold water.

5   Remove from heat and let cool and then carefully strain the stock. Like the chicken stock, this can be kept refrigerated for 3 days or frozen. Follow the same directions as in step 6 of the chicken stock recipe.

Roasted Vegetable Stock

Makes 2 quarts

2 tablespoons olive oil

3 carrots peeled – cut into 1-inch pieces

3 stalks celery – cut into 1-inch pieces

1 large onion – quartered with peel intact

2 leeks – cleaned and quartered

4 cloves whole garlic – peeled

3 quarts of water

1 medium tomato – quartered

2 sprigs thyme

2 teaspoon of salt

3 good turns of fresh ground pepper

1   Preheat oven to 350 degrees.

2   Pour the olive oil into a large roasting pan. Place the carrots, celery, onions, leeks and garlic into the pan, toss to coat with the olive oil and then roast for 45 minutes.

3   Fill a 4-quart stockpot, three-quarters full with cold water, and then add the roasted vegetables, tomato, parsley, thyme, salt and pepper. Simmer for 45 minutes. Let the stock cool before straining. Note: A vegetable stock is generally best used within 24 hours, unless you are freezing it.

Creating this book, indeed creating the cooking school, has been not only a labor of love, good food and wine, but one that would have been impossible if it were not for the constant support, encouragement and love of many, many people, our friends and families. There are many people we wish to thank.

The school opened with Katie Scott, to whom we say a big thank you for helping get Montecito Country Kitchen off the ground. A big thank you also goes to all the hundreds of students who have shared all the meals we have taught since 1999.

Special thanks to Marie Larkin, who not only got the word out in Santa Barbara about the school when it first opened, and has endlessly talked about it to everyone she knows, but also insisted on our meeting each other. Because of that meeting, a great friendship was formed, the school developed and the partnership blossomed to celebrate the foods of France, Italy and the Mediterranean.

To Julia Child, an enormous thank you for your inspiration and encouragement.

Special thanks also go to Alyce Faye Cleese, our diehard supporter, student and promoter of this book, whose continued encouragement and enthusiasm pushed us past just dreaming about it and has helped it come to fruition. To Leesa Wilson-Goldmuntz; merci, merci, grazie, grazie, for being there since the beginning, supplying champagne at all the best times and for introducing us to Media 27.

To Teri, Melinda M, Melinda G, Susan, Alison P., Alison L., Elena, Michael F., Dinah and Win, Jennifer and Rob, Jen, our regulars, neighbors and friends, a huge thank you for your continued support of the school and all our endeavors.

To Tricia Fountaine, what can we say? Your flowers which adorn our dining tables and the photos in this book are always magnificent. A thousand thank yous to you for always being willing to pitch in.

To Tony Princiotta, Norbert Wabnig and everyone at The Cheese Store in Beverly Hills, grazie and danke for nearly two decades of friendship, fabulous cheese and teaching the delicious 'Cheese Store' class with us in every series since we opened.

Thank you to our local suppliers, farmers and purveyors of fine foods: Kanaloa Seafood for all the delicious fish; Shalhoob Meat Company for all their fine cuts; to Jim, Maria, Gloria, Rosie and Michael of Pudwill Farms for their fantastic berries; to David Lelande for the bountiful fruit; to Bob at Lazy Acres for pairing wines with all our menus; to Peacock Farms for the best eggs on the West Coast; to Fairview Gardens for their divine white asparagus and organic goodies; and to Henry Mancini of A & M Mushrooms for all your great tubers.

Photographs by Monique Fay, Pascale Beale-Groom, Jeff Litherland, Mike Verbois and Shukri Farhad

To Michael Knuckey, thank you for teaching with us and bringing an Australian flavor and much laughter to the classes.

To Rick and Ro Sanders, for hosting the first class we taught together in their lovely home and for sharing all their foodie passions with us over the years.

To Monique Fay, an enormous MERCI for having the school invade her home for two series and for all her beautiful photography which has so evocatively illustrated this book.

To Media 27, Mike, Shukri, Judi, Jeff and Ruth: thank you for your energy, creativity, and colorful vision in transforming our working model into the fabulous book we have today. The photographs are marvelous too. This book would not have been possible without you.

To Peter Beale, Melinda Mars and Michele McGovern-Gilbert whom we thank profusely for painstakingly proofreading this book again and again and again.

And to our families, especially Scott, Steven, Stephanie, Fabrizio, Emily, William, Olivia, Alexandre, Monique and Peter, who have put up with our rantings and ravings, myriad of tastings and culinary adventures over the past two years as we have tested, changed, retested and redeveloped recipes. You have been the backbone of this project. Thank you for your patience and allowing us to have the necessary time to realize this dream.

For Ann Marie, without whom Montecito Country Kitchen could not have become the great cooking school that it is today: You arrived like a whirlwind, bringing your trademark Italian flavor with you. Your spontaneity, creativity, and your enthusiasm is infectious, as is your sense of humor which has enlivened all of our classes. Thank you for showing me the lighter side of things and teaching me that I don't have to dice everything I do into tiny little pieces!   —PASCALE

For Pascale, my partner in cream: For sharing your dream with me and for always supporting me no matter how Guido I became! For without you I would not be writing this cookbook. Pascale, you are truly an inspirational person, not only in the kitchen but in every aspect of your life and I thank you for bringing out the creativity in me.   —ANN MARIE